The Mental Health

Recovery

Hand Book

by

Bruce Dolan Smith

2nd Edition

Published by BDS Distributors

Copyright 2018 by BDS Distributors

Table of Contents

Introduction

I have lived with mental illness all my life. I've heard of the word recovery however I never thought it was possible. I had many hospitalizations over the years. I have leaned first hand everything I know about mental illness. I am presently going for my associates degree in psych and rehabilitation. It took a long time until I was finally placed on the mediations I take today to maintain my recovery. I can remember one hospitalization years ago we had a guest speaker from N.A.M.I. come to see us. She started to tell us her story how she was able to go back go to college and enter the ministry and boy I thought to myself I wish I could do that. At the time, I did not think it was possible. I thought I was going to be like I was the rest of my life. It took years and hard work to get where I am today. I thank all the doctors and staff that has helped me over the years. Also, I have a very good support system. I have many friends to help me when I ask for help.

I hope this book helps you also to realize that there is such as word as recovery. You do not have to be the way you are the rest of your life. It takes time and hard work to overcome your illness. You can do it just take one day at a time

and sometimes even one second at a time.

Chapter 1

Do people really recover from mental illness?

Mental illness is just like any other illness. It takes time and patients to overcome, first off, we must accept the illness whether it be physical or psychological. Once we accept the illness then it is time to move forward. I can remember when I first got sick I thought it was physical. It took me three years and many different doctors and test until I finally came to accept my illness was psychological. I was in the hospital and the doctor was going to release me however I still felt the same way I came in. No better. He had a psychiatrist come and see me. The next day I was transferred to their behavior ward. It was not until that time was I ready to accept I had a mental illness. The first day I was there I was in a group listening to the patients talk and described their symptoms. Each symptom sounded just like I was having. They were depressed and having anxiety attacks. I was in there for ten days and put on some medications for anxiety and depression. I started to feel better. It took time, but I was on the road to recovery.

It was not until I moved back to New Jersey in 2000 did I make a lot of progress. I saw a psychiatrist and she recommend for me to attend their partial day care center. I would be there

from 9am to 3pm. The first part of the morning

we would be put into different work groups such

as: cleaning, snack bar, sorting out coupons.

Then the second part of the day they had

different types of groups for depression, anxiety,

loss, grief, and many different groups which

helped me to work thru my issues and problems.

Chapter 2

The definition of recovery

According to www.dictionary.com recovery

is defined as follows:

1. an act of recovering.

2. the regaining of or possibility of regaining

something lost or taken away.

3. restoration or return to health from sickness.

4. restoration or return to any former and better

state or condition.

I was watching a video on you tube by

Mental Health Recovery & Resiliency Principles

& Practices Part one and they had two definitions of recovery.

"Recovery is a process of readjusting our attitudes, feelings, perceptions, and beliefs about ourselves, others and life in general. It is a process of self-discovery, self-renewal, and transformation. Recovery is deeply emotional. It transcends the particular issue itself."

Leroy Spaniol

"Recovery is living a satisfying, hopeful and contributing life even with limitations caused by illness. Recovery involves the development of new meaning and purpose in one's life as one

grows beyond the catastrophic effects on mental
illness."

William Anthony

Mental illness is biological, psychological,
social, spiritual, cultural, and environmental.
As you work thru these barriers you will find
you will start to feel better. We need to take our
medication to help the biological aspect of our
illness. Then thru therapy whether it be group or
individual therapy is where we work thru the
problems that may be bothering us. The social
aspect is to help us to get out of the house and
socialize. This is where you may be able to find
additional support and make some new friends.

As we seek the spiritual part of us we ask for

God to help us thru our dark days. There may be

some days that are hard for you to get out. This

is when you really need to go to a group or be

around people. The more you do this the easier

it will become. I have to lose weight and

recently I made a pack with myself that I was

going to walk a certain number of steps each

day. I like to walk in our parks near where I

live. Towards the end of the day if I do not

meet the number of steps I want to take then I

will just walk inside of my apartment until I

meet the number of steps I want to take for that

day. In the beginning, it was hard for me to do

however it is becoming naturally for me. The same for you in the beginning you may find it hard to go out and meet with people but the more you do it the easier it will get. Trust and have faith in God that he will see you thru these hard days and they will become easier for you to do.

Chapter 3

Having a support system

It is very important that you have a support system. Have a least five people who you can call when you need to. They can be a family member, friend, or a health care professional.

Develop a support plan should your symptoms start to come back. It is very important that you make a list of people who you can call should you start to feel your symptoms start to come back. By catching this early could help your illness from getting worse.

Also, there are support groups for all types of illnesses all over the country. Ask your doctor where there is one in your area. It is good for you to share whatever is on your mind in these groups. You might want to find a self-help center in your area. I belong to a self-help center in my area. They have a living room, library, kitchen, computer room and an exercise room. They have a meal once a day at dinner time. The center has different groups during the week where you can share your experience with mental illness. This helped me when I first moved up here from Florida. I started to go and would go to the different groups they had to offer. After a while I got job there picking up the members and taking them home. Also, I worked as a facilitator which to me is an assistant manager. This helped me get on the road to recovery. There were days that if I did not have the center to go to I would just stay in bed. We all know when this happens it will just lead to a viscous cycle. It is good to get out among people to keep yourself active and your mind off whatever is bothering you.

Chapter 4

Changes in Your Life Style

Having a mental illness is just like having any other type of illness. There may be changes you will have to make in your life style. This may mean by taking medications, seeing a psychiatrists or therapist. I remember when I first accepted I had a mental illness meant I had to make changes in my daily routine. This meant by not staying in bed like I was used to. I had to go to a partial day care center for a while. I was not used to attending groups, so this was all new to me. At first, I just kept quiet and did not share but after a while I started to open up.

My doctor told me to walk and get some exercises in during the day. This helped me not only psychological but also physically. By walking or doing any type of exercise helps the chemistry in our brain.

I had to get use to taking mediations daily which is very important.

Take time in your day to do some fun activities. I myself like to go for a walk, write, read, take a bus strip, watch a good movie, play the organ. When I am busy I do not have time to dwell on things that are bothering me. When I am feeling depressed, sad or anxious I try to find something to keep me busy.

What activities makes you feel better?

How do you feel before you do these activities?

How do you feel after the activities?

Take a break, schedule some time for fun. If you have a pet take time and play with it, listen to music, exercise, go swimming, dance, community sports, such as: football, baseball or basketball. Other fun things to do:

- Go to a park and watch the wildlife

- Do some gardening

- Visit with friends

- Volunteer work

- Visit museums

- Cook

- Watch a movie

- Go on a You Tube Marathon. Find some interesting videos

- Write a daily blog

There are so many things that you can do to have fun. This will bring life back into your world.

Have you heard the expression laughter is the best medicine? Researchers have found that laughter is a good treatment for anxiety attacks. When we laugh our lungs are filled up with fresh air and we breath out the stale air that are in our lungs. Find some things that makes you laugh. Perhaps a good comedy or watch Americas Funniest Videos.

If you do not have one get a pet. Pets are good to have because they are always there even when you are in a bad mood. Our pets love us unconditionally. They can make us laugh. Petting your pet can be relaxing. Pets help relieve stress and tension. It does not matter how good pets are for most people some people

may not like pets. This is ok, it is a personal

choice.

Chapter 5

Coping Skills

Coping skills are tools used to help manage an illness. They vary from person to person and illness to illness. Coping skills can be creative, physical, musical, spiritual, or can even fit into another category. They often take time to develop and get used to doing. It is worth it overall. They can make a significant contribution to one's symptom management.

Mental illness is just like any other illness. There are ways we can cope with it once we are able to accept our illness. By developing good coping skills will help you get by each day and

teach you different ways to cope with your

illness whether it be mental or physical. Once I

accepted my illness was psychological and not

physical I started to think ways I can cope with

my illness. First, I had to think of what did I like

to do before I got sick. Then I wrote each one

down. I took advice from others of ways they

coped with their illness. Here is the list I made,

perhaps you will find some on the list that will

help you.

1. I would read a book

2. Take a shower

3. Listen to music

4. Watching TV

5. Journaling

6. Called some friends on the phone

7. Cry

8. Color

9. Draw

10. Worked on my books

11. Read my bible

12. Walked

13. Exercise

14. Cleaning

15. Prayed

Make a list of ways you think you may be able to cope with your illness.

Set time aside for yourself to do something fun. It may be watching a funny movie, calling a friend on the phone who you haven't talked to in a long time, and other things you once enjoyed before you got sick.   By keeping active keeps your mind from not thinking of negative thoughts. It is the negative thoughts that gets us into trouble. Keep positive no matter how hard it may be. Make a list of pros and cons of an issue you are having. Talk to your therapist perhaps he or she may have some advice they can give you.

Remember the important thing is to keep your mind active it is when we sit and think of all our problems your depression will just get worse. I enjoy listening to music so when I am resting I will put on music from the 70's or 80's. I like to listen to Christian music it is up lifting and puts my mind at ease.

The key thing is do not dwell on the negative thoughts instead try to think and keep positive.

Chapter 6

Self-Esteem

The definition of self-esteem according to

dictionary.com is:

1. a realistic respect for or favorable impression

of oneself; self-respect.

2. an inordinately or exaggeratedly favorable

impression of oneself.

Self-Esteem is how you think and feel about

yourself. It is your sense of self-worth, how

valuable and a worthy a person you are. People

who have a high self-esteem feels good about

themselves. Then on the other hand people who

have a low self-esteem feels just the opposite,
how bad they feel about them self's.

You want to be around positive people.
People who feel good about themselves and
others.   When you surround yourself around
negative people then you will become negative
like them.

Do not worry about what the next guy thinks
of you. Think of what others say and how you
feel about yourself. You can build up your self-
esteem by looking around you and what you
have accomplished or perhaps you helped
someone today. Remember keep positive when

the negative self-talk comes back just turn it
around and turn it into something positive.

Today for some reason I feel kind of
off in a way. This morning I got a lot of work
done in my house. I did some cleaning and
worked on this book I am writing now. I was
laying down and that old depression wanted to
come back. That was when I said No, and I got
up did a few more things and started writing
again. See it is how we handle the negative talk
we get from our selves. If it was the old me I
would have slipped back into a deep depression.
You cannot let this happen. Think to yourself
how far you have gotten since you first got sick.

You still have a mental illness, but it does not control you any longer. Self-esteem doesn't only come from what others say about us, but it also comes from what we think about ourselves. Sad to say if you have a friend who continuing talking negative about you that person is not your friend. It is time to move on and find another friend. A friend who is going to be a friend to you instead of your worst enemy not realizing.

Having a good self-esteem is important to all of us. When we think good about our self and we have good self-esteem then recovery is possible.

You are a good person. Pat yourself on the back

When does poor self-esteem happens? It could have come from years ago. Perhaps you had a teacher that was very critical, your brother or sister, friends and even ads on the television. Think back and see if you can tell when you started to think negative about yourself.   I can remember my parents never encourage my sister or I to go to college.

Answer some of these questions about yourself:

- What are your feelings about yourself right now?

- Are they negative or positive?

- Write down on a piece of paper one side the negative feelings and on the other side the positive feelings you have about yourself.

- Where did you get the negative feeling from?

How can you break the cycle of negative self-talk? First take a look at what you are telling yourself. Look at the negative side. Now turn that negative into something positive. Below are a few examples:

- I can't do anything right.

- I can do things right and I do.

- I am a bad person

- No, I'm not I am a good person

- No one likes me

- This is wrong I do know people who like me

- I am stupid

- I am smart

Now use the following space to write down your negative thoughts on one side and your positive thoughts on the other side:

<u>Negative Thought</u>   <u>Positive Thought</u>

In the above exercise now write down the negative thoughts and turn them into positive thoughts.

<u>Negative thoughts</u>   <u>Positive thoughts</u>

How can you build your self-esteem?

1. Do something you enjoy doing

2. Watch a funny movie

3. Give yourself a treat. You deserve it.

4. Visit or call a friend you haven't spoken

    to in a while.

5. Write down things that you accomplished

    at the end of each day.

6. Feel good about yourself

7. Push the negative thoughts aside and put a

    positive thought in place of it.

8. Go for a walk

9. Keep up with your personal hygiene.

10.Celebrate that you have been given

another day.

These are just a few ways that you can build

up your self-esteem. It is very important that we

think good about ourselves. It is when we have

poor self-esteem our depression comes back

Chapter 7

Affirmations

What are affirmations? Affirmations are

positive statements that describe a situation or

goal. These are words that will encourage you

to get onto the road to recovery. Make a list for

yourself. Below are a few examples:

- I am worthwhile

- I am loved

- I am forgiven

- I forgive

- I have hope

- I have faith

- I am honest

- I like myself

- God has a plan for me

- I can take care of my self

- I am a good person

- I am not a bad person

- I am at peace with my Higher Power

- I will only think positive about myself

Keep a list of positive affirmations by you.

Everything a negative thought comes look at

your sheet and read your affirmations.

Chapter 8

Journaling

Writing a journal is a way of ventilating. It helps you to write down things that are either on your mind or what is going on at the time.

Journaling is an important tool for the road to recovery. It is very simple you do not have to worry about how it is written or punctuation points. This is for you and only you. If you decide you want to share it with someone then that is ok.

First off to start you will need paper and a pencil or pen. Start to brain storm and write down what is going on at the moment. Set aside

a certain time each day for you to take out a few

minutes and write in your journal. Write how

your day is going and perhaps any symptoms

you may be having.

By journaling may help you in the following

ways:

- What causes your depression, anxiety, or

  panic attacks?

- A guide to help you on the road to

  recovery

- Write down your own personal history

- Help you in problem solving

- Keep track of your cycle of your moods

- Help understand what is affecting your moods

- Help you grieve over a loss of a love one

- Help explore your dreams

- Help you get in touch with your true feelings

- To pinpoint any stressors that are going on in your life at that moment

By journaling it can help you in many ways to help you on the road to recovery. It is your personal journal. It is up to you to decide if you are going to show it to anyone. Keep it in a safe place but where it is handy for you to get to. You may be

on the road or even forgot to take your

journal with you that is ok. Just write

down on a piece of paper what you

wanted to write. You can later write it in

your journal.

Journaling Goals:

- Help understand why I get depressed

- What may be causing my anxiety?

- Track changes in my moods

- Work on problems that are bothering me

- Help keep track of my dreams

- Help to pinpoint my stressors

- The best thing that happened to me today

- What made me feel low today?

- What made me feel high today?

- Take a personal inventory

- Things I want to work on to maintain my

  mental health

  You are on the road to recovery

Journaling is a good way to vent. By writing

down things that are on you mind you do not

keep things in side of you. Just think of a

pressure cooker. As it boils it is letting off

steam. If you do not turn down the heat

eventually it is going to explode. This is what

happens to us if we hold back anything that is
bothering us.

Start today. It would be good if you can get a
book with blank pages in it. Go into a quiet
space and sit back and relax. Start to write down
anything that is on your mind. It is also a good
idea to find someone you can talk to. However,
there are some things that you do not want to
share with anyone. This is when journaling
comes in handy.

As you journal you will be able to keep track
of how you are feeling on a daily basis. You can
note in your journal if you are feeling depressed,
anxiety, or if you have had a manic episode for

those that are Bi Polar. It is a good idea if you are seeing a therapist to keep a journal of your work with in your session.

Find a safe space where you can keep your journal. You will want to find a space where people will not be able to find it. This is personal and only for you. You may decide however at some point you may want to share your writings with someone. This is up to you.

As far as rules in writing a journal the fun part is there are no rules. This is for you and you make the rules. You do not have to worry about spelling, penmanship, grammar, punctuation points or neatness. If you can set aside a certain time each day for journaling. The time is up to you. If you miss a day that is ok just pick up where you left off.

Below are some examples of what you may want to put into your journal:

- How are you feeling?

- Your mood

- What made you feel depressed today?

- What is making you feel good today?

- If you have an anxiety attack write what caused it if you know.

- What was the stressors of your day?

- What was the highlight of the day?

- What was your low point of the day.

Chapter 9

Rule out medical causes of your illness

In the beginning of your illness you will want to see your doctor and tell him the symptoms you are having. He may want to have some tests done to rule out any physical reasons for your symptoms. I remember when I first got sick back in the 90's I had all sorts of symptoms. Sometimes is felt like I was having a heart attack. I went to my medical doctor at first and he did all sorts of test. All my test came back normal. I still was not satisfied, I still thought my problem was physical even though my doctor told me it was not. He advised me to see a psychiatrist, that he thought I was having anxiety

attacks along with depression. I still did not

listen to him. I would either call the ambulance

or take myself to the emergency room. Once

again, they ran a lot of test and all of them came

back normal. This went on for three years. I

went to many different doctors and each one told

me the same. It was not until I was hospitalized,

and my doctor had a psychiatrist come in and

see me. She advised me to go be transferred to

their behavior ward. I was in there for ten days.

The first day I was in there I went to the groups

they had during the day. As I listen to each

person describe their symptoms I started to

think. The symptoms they were having was the same as what I was having. They were having anxiety and panic attacks also, they were suffering from depression. Now finally was I able to accept my illness as being psychological. I was put on new medication for anxiety and depression. After a few weeks, I started to feel better. It was an uphill battle for many years until I was finally placed on the right medications. Mental illness is not like having a broken arm. The doctors cannot just put you on certain medications and say that is the cure. It takes time and being on different combination of medications until they can find the right ones that are suitable for you. When you first see a psychiatrist he or she will ask you a lot of questions. Also pending on the symptoms, you are having what medications they will try you on at first. They will see how you do and if you are getting better then perhaps they found the right combination.

The main thing is to come to terms with acceptance. Acceptance is a long word and a hard one to accept. Once you realize your illness is not physical then perhaps some of your anxiety will go away. I can remember when I felt like I was having a heart attack it was at its worse in the beginning. Once I got in the emergency room I started to feel better. After

the doctor told me the result of my test most if

not all the symptoms disappeared.

The brain can cause a lot of illnesses. The

key thing is yes go to a medical doctor to rule

out anything physical then if all your test come

back normal see a psychiatrist.

Chapter 10

Taking Medications

Taking medications for psychological reasons

is just like taking medications for psychical

illnesses. It is important because the

medications will help you maintain your illness.

You may have side effects from the medication.

Be sure to tell your doctor what side affects you

are having. Some side effects are normal.

Some psychotropic medications can cause

weight gain. There are ways to battle this.

Watch what you eat. If you are hungry eat

something that is healthy. This will help you

from gaining weight. Also exercising is good to
help control the weight gain. Even if you just
walk each day. When I was first put on psych
medications I gained about thirty pounds. I
started to watch what I ate and started walking
every day.

Remember taking medications for
psychological reasons is just as important taking
medications for any other illnesses. Talk to your
doctor about what ever side affects you are
having.

Chapter 11

Treatments and Therapies

Mental Health has come a long way since

the 50's. There are new medications, treatments

and therapies.

Below you will find the different types of

treatments and therapies:

Psychotherapy or talk therapy is when a

person talks about difficulties in coping with

everyday life. A person may discuss to their

therapist the impact of trauma, medical illness or

loss, death of a loved, and specific mental

disorders like depression or anxiety.

Psychotherapies is a way for the person to discuss mental illness and emotional difficulties. It can help eliminate or control troubling symptoms. This hopefully will help the person function better and increase well-being and healing.

Problems helped by psychotherapy include difficulties in coping with daily life; the impact of trauma, medical illness or loss, like the death of a loved one; and specific mental disorders, like depression or anxiety. There are several different types of psychotherapy and some types may work better with certain problems or issues.

Psychotherapy may be used in combination with
medication or other therapies.

It is a good idea for you to find a self-help
center in your area. They usually have different
types of groups where you can listen to the
people's different experiences with their illness.
When you are ready to you also can share. I go
to Better Future Self Help Center here is
Washington NJ. They have a Bi Polar group
every Tuesday. It is help full for me because I
can relate to the people in the group. I listen to
their experiences.

There are also online groups such as DBSA

has an online support group throughout the

week. This is good for the people who cannot

get out and attend meetings.

Chapter 12

Staying well

It is important for you to make a plan on what helps you maintain your illness. As I have gone over in previous chapters staying on your medications is very important. If there are any changes in your symptoms it is also important that you tell your doctor.

Last year I had a lot of losses in my life. I did not realize it at the time however my symptoms started to come back. I was very tired and fatigue, wanted to sleep all the time and started to get withdrawn. Once again, I thought it was due to a medical illness. I went to

my doctor and had a lot of tests done. Most of

my tests came back normal. My blood pressure

was very high I also had some problems with my

stomach. I was in the hospital a couple of times

due to my high blood pressure. I had tests done

on my heart again being heart disease runs in the

family and I am a diabetic. The tests came back

good on my heart so basically my depression

came back again. This time once all my tests

came back normal I knew what I had to do. My

blood pressure started to come down with the

medications I was put on. The psychiatrists I

was seeing was not doing anything for me, so I

researched a doctor who specializes in Chronic

Fatigue Syndrome. I found one, but he was an

hour away from me. I made an appointment

with him and I was able to see him in a few

days. Right away he made some changes in my

psych medications. It did not happen right away

however after a few weeks I started to feel

better. I moved out of where I was living at and

got an apartment with a friend of mine. The

people who I lived with before had a lot of

problems with drinking and fighting. I did not

realize it at the time but that was affecting me.

Within a few months after I moved out I started

to feel better. My blood pressure was getting

better. I was on a sleep medication which the new psychiatrist said that could also be causing me to be tired during the day. So, he took me off that and replaced it with an anti-anxiety medication. I am feeling much better now.

Sometimes we have to make changes in our life in order to help us to either get better with our illness or maintain a healthy life. If you are going thru some health problems or your symptoms are coming back look around you and see if there has been any changes in your life. I did not realize it but last year when I had all the losses it did bother me.

So, it is very important that you tell your

doctor everything that is going on. Tell him or

her what symptoms you are having and how

severe it is. Communication is important with

all your doctors and support system that you

have.

Chapter 13

Stay in the present

You do not want to go back to the past. If you had issues such as: abuse, trauma, illness, death of a love one and more try to focus on the present. By living in the past will only put a hold on your recovery. You may want to work with your therapist on issues had in your past. Think of the progress you have made. You cannot change things in your past you can only move forward by putting them aside. It is ok to think of the good memories of your past. I know around the holidays are hard for some people because they lost loved ones. I get depressed around the holidays but when that happens I think of the good memories of my past.

We as humans tend to live in the past or the future. Also, we spend a lot of time in the future projecting what may happened. This causes us a lot of worry because we think of what may happen even though it may not.   Live in the present you cannot do anything that you did in the past.

If you find yourself drifting in the past or the future, try to focus on what is right in front you. Focus on positive things in your life right now. Continue to focus on the present. By doing this it will train your mind to stop thinking about the past and the future, instead you will be focusing on the present and be able to live in the moment.

Focus on your breathing. Take some deep breaths. Breath thru your nose exhale out of your mouth. Do this for a few minutes and focus on your breathing. Now you are ready to come back to the present. You may want to do these exercises as you feel like you are drifting off in the past or the future.

It is ok to reminisce about your past thinking pleasant thoughts and think about the future. The key thing is just do not live in them. Stay in the present.

Chapter 14

Work Sheets

We all have bad days it depends on how we deal with those days when they come up. We can sit and think about it but it will just get worse.

Answer the following questions and when you start to feel bad go to these questions and read them to yourself.

- What are ten things that you are grateful for?

- What would a perfect day be like for you?

- What is the best complement someone said to you?

- What did you like to do as a child that made you happy?

Chapter 15

Preventing Depression

To me depression is like living in a dark
tunnel with no end. Back when I first got sick I
never thought I would see day light at the end of
my tunnel. It took time and a lot of work, but I
did get better. When I moved back here to New
Jersey in 2000 I went to a partial day care
program. It was for people with mental illness.
At first, I went five days week from 9am to 3pm.
They had different groups during the day. This
was when I could work thru all my problems.
My mother had just passed away, so I was

dealing with grieving her loss. I also saw a

psychiatrist while I was going to the program.

The best ways you can try to prevent

depression is to talk about your problems with a

friend, relative or a therapist. Holding things in

just makes matters worse. Be sure to take your

medications as prescribed from your doctor.

Exercise is a good way to release chemicals

in the brain which produces positive emotions.

It helps fight stress, depression, and anxiety. It

can be hard in the beginning to keep a daily

routine. Once you start it will get easier. I walk

every day. On my cell phone, I have an app that

keeps track of how many steps I have taken.

Right now, I cannot do a lot however I try to
maintain 2500 steps for the day. This is not
much by far however because of my Chronic
Fatigue Syndrome I have to be careful that I do
not over do it.

Get enough sleep each night. People with
depression can either get too much sleep or not
sleep enough. By not getting the right amount of
sleep each night can worsen the depression. If
you have problems getting to sleep talk to your
doctor, perhaps he or she can advise you what to
do. There are medications which help to fall
asleep. By getting the correct amount of sleep
will help your depression.

If you drink alcohol you really need to stop. Alcohol is a natural depressant which could be the cause of your depression. Also, it is not good to mix any alcoholic beverage with medications.

Meditation can help someone with depression. Sit back and relax, sit in a comfortable position. Breathe through your nose and exhale through your mouth. Just focus on your breathing. Perhaps you can have some quiet music on. Take time out of your day to do this as often as you can. If you have problems falling asleep this should help you. The key thing is to relax.

Enjoy your life, have fun. What do you like to do to have fun? Have you ever gone bowling, bicycle ride, walk in the parks? There are many more things you can do to have fun. You can go to the movies. Get out of the house even if it is just to go to the mall. You do not have to buy anything. This is a good way you can exercise. The key thing it to keep busy and keep your mind occupied. If you just sit around the house your depression will only get worse. Continuing thinking about your problems will not solve them. Enjoy your life, have fun.

Have a pet. Depending on your situation is what kind of pet you would to have. Cats and dogs take on some responsibly and expense.

Fish on the other hand are easy to take care of

and are very therapeutic. You do not want to

take on too much responsibility. You may have

a pet already. That's great.

   Ask your doctor if you should take any

vitamins some may help with depression.

However, like any other medication you want to

consult your doctor first.

   Set yourself goals for the day. Try to make a

list of things you would like to accomplish for

the week and break it down. Prioritize your list,

then make a list for each day of the week. If you

do not get one thing done, then that is ok just put

it on the next day's list. Make sure you do not
overdue yourself. It is better to get small tasks
done each day. Be sure your goals are
achievable.

Try to keep positive. I know it is easier said
than done some days. I sometimes have the
habit of thinking the worse. This can affect the
way I feel both physically and psychologically.
It is better to talk to someone about your
problems. Perhaps they may have a good
suggestion or perhaps it just be the way you are
thinking at that particular moment. Remember
think positive!

Chapter 16

When is it time to call your Doctor?

By all means if you feel you need to talk to your doctor and it is not on this list please call anyway. This is only a guide line

- Think of harming yourself or others

- Hearing voices

- Thoughts of suicide or you know of someone who has mentioned wanting to commit suicide.

Warning signs of suicide include

- Use of illegal drugs or drinking alcohol heavily

- Talking, writing, or drawing about
  death, including writing suicide notes,
  and speaking of items that can cause
  physical harm such as pills, guns, or
  knives.

- Spending long periods of time alone

- Giving away possessions

- Aggressive behavior or suddenly
  appearing calm

Be alert

- Be on guard may be enough should your
  mood change. If your mood does not
  improve call your doctor.

- If you have a friend or a loved one and he
  or she is experiencing a manic episode
  and behaving irrationally have the person
  seek help.

Positive things you can do

- Get counseling

- Go to some type of group therapy

- Talk about your problems

- Find a self-help center in your area

Chapter 17

Tips on Preventing Relapse

It is very important that if you start to feel depressed make an appointment with your doctor or therapist. Focus on positive things that you do have in your life. Think of something that you enjoy doing. If you can do it start it right away. This will help get your mind off your depression. The problem is sometimes if we do not confront the issue we become like a boiling pot. Eventually we will explode.

Last thing you want to think about is, am I going to relapse? I was doing great for over ten years. Then suddenly I had something happen to me and my depression came back again. I recognized the warning signs and knew I was headed for trouble. I went to the emergency room and told the doctor how I felt. Right away I was admitted to their behavior ward. At first, I felt like a failure because I thought I would never relapse. Things happens in our life that we have no control over. The important thing is realizing your symptoms. It is ok to ask for help.

Below is an action plan on relapse prevention:

1. Write down any events or situations that has triggered relapses in the past.

2. What are the early warning signs that you have had in the past?

3. What has helped you before when you have experienced early warning signs?

4. Make a list of people who has helped you and what you would like for them to do for you now.

5. Make a list of friends or family that you would like to have contact in case of an emergency.

Below is a plan if you should be in crisis

1. What can I do if I am in crisis?

2. Ways I can help to relieve stress.

3. People I can call on when I am in crisis.

4. What support groups I can call on when I am in crisis

Chapter 18

What is Bi Polar Disorder?

Bi-polar Disorder is known as manic

depressive disorder years ago. It is an illness

which the patient has extremes highs then

extremes lows. The patient mood changes

which alternates between manic episodes of

abnormally high energy and it reverse to

extreme lows of depression.

People who are diagnosed with bi-polar may

have it so severe that they may not be able to

function at work, in family or social situations,

or in relationships with others. This illness can

become so severe where the person can become

suicidal.

What causes Bi-polar disorder?

It has not been known yet what the exact cause

of bipolar is. Researchers has found that it can

run in families. It can also be affected by

persons living environment or family situation.

There is a chemical imbalance in the brain can

be another cause.

A person having sleep deprivation or substance

abuse, including caffeine can cause a manic

episode. Initially stress may be a trigger in depression or mania. However, as the illness progresses, mood swings may not be caused by any specific event. Without treatment, your bipolar disorder may get worse, causing you to cycle more frequently between mania and depression.

What are the symptoms?

When a person develops bipolar they may have the following symptoms:

- Be abnormally happy
- Increased physical and mental activity and energy

- Racing thoughts, racing speech, flight ideas

- Be Irritable for a week or more

- Aggressive behavior

- Spend a lot of money

- Grandiose delusions, inflated sense of self-importance

- Impulsiveness, poor judgment, distractibility

- Get involved in dangerous activities

- Be sleep deprived

- Decreased need for sleep without experiencing fatigue

- Feel extremely happy or very irritable

- Have a high opinion of them selves

- No need of sleep as usual

- Very talkative

- Be more active than usual

- Difficulty concentrating due to having too

  many thoughts at once (racing thoughts)

- Be easily distracted by sights and sounds.

- Act impulsively on reckless things, such

  as go on shopping sprees, drive recklessly,

  get into foolish business ventures, or have

  frequent, indiscriminate, or unsafe sex.

Depression may cause a person to:

- Feel sad or anxious for a significant time

- Feel hopeless or pessimistic or worthlessness

- Feelings of guilt

- Have slowed thoughts and speech due to low energy.

- Have difficulty concentrating remembering and making decisions

- Have changes in eating and sleeping habits leading to too much or too little eating sleeping

- Have decreased interest in usual activities including sex

- Having suicidal thoughts.

- Prolonged sadness or unexplained crying

  spells

- Irritability, anger, worry, agitation,

  anxiety

- Loss of energy, persistent lethargy

- Unexplained aches and pains

- Does not take pleasure in former interest,

  social withdrawal.

- Excessive drinking alcohol or use of

  chemical substances

After the manic episode passes, the person may return to normal, but their mood may swing in the opposite direction of feelings of sadness, depression, and hopelessness. When they are depressed, they may have trouble concentrating, remembering, and making decisions; have changes in their eating and sleeping habits; and lose interest in things they once enjoyed.

A person's mood can change suddenly from mild to extreme. They may develop it gradually over several days or weeks. After a person has a manic episode they may return to normal or their mood may swing in the opposite direction and feel useless, hopeless, and extremely sad.

When the person feels depressed they may have trouble concentrating, remembering, and making decisions; having changes in their eating and sleeping habits. They lose interest in things they once enjoyed. Some people do become suicidal or harm themselves during episodes of depression. Some feel as if they cannot move, care, or think.

Bipolar disorder is a very complex illness. It is because there are many phases and symptoms. There is no one lab tests for the disorder. The doctor or therapist will ask the patient detail questions about what kind of symptoms they have had and how long it has lasted. In order to come up with the correct diagnose. A patient must have had a manic episode lasting a week (less if they had to be hospitalized). During the same time, the patient must have had three or more specific symptoms of mania such needing less sleep, being more talkative, behaving wildly or irresponsibly in activities that could have serious outcomes, or feeling as if your thought is racing.

Treatment:

  Treatment is first done by medications to manage the manic episodes and periods depressions. The doctor may have to try several medications until finding the right combination to manage the symptoms long-term. The

medications included are mood stabilizers along

with antipsychotics. Antidepressants are used

carefully for episodes of depression, because

they cause some people to cycle into a manic

phase.

 Hospitalization may be needed while the

person is in the extreme mode of the illness.

This is to protect them from hurting themselves

or others.

Along with medication another tool which

will help in the treatment is counseling. A

patient may want to find themselves a good

counselor along with having a psychiatrist. Also

find a good self-help group for whatever their

illness is. It is the best place for them to get

support. For example, if they are bipolar have

them look in their area to see where there is a

bipolar group. If they cannot find one ask their

doctor, or counselor. If they have a computer

lookup bipolar, they will be amazed on what

they can find on it.

Key concepts in recovery:

✓ Hope. By managing symptoms, it is

possible for the patient to experience long

periods of wellness. By believing you can

cope with your mood disorder is both

accurate and essential in recovery.

✓ Perspective. Both Bi Polar and depression

often follow cyclical patterns. Sometimes

by going thru painful times it is difficult to

believe that things will get better. The

main thing is Do Not Give Up.

✓ Personal Responsibility. It is up to you to

keep your mood stabilized You need to

take your medications as prescribed, keep

your doctor and therapist appointments

and ask for help from others if you need it.

✓ Self-Advocacy. Be an advocate for

yourself by learning about your disorder,

ask questions, learn from your peers.

✓ Education. You can never stop learning
about mental illness. There are new
medications and treatments coming out
each day. By learning about your illness,
you can not only help yourself, but you
can help others.

✓ Support. Get yourself a good support
system. You may want to include your
friends, family, therapist and your doctors.

Chapter 19

What is Anxiety?

Anxiety is a normal reaction to stress. It is nature's way of your mind and body's way to respond to events that are threating you. Everyone experiences anxiety at some point in their life it depends on how you cope when in tense situations. Anxiety usually goes away when whatever triggered it is over. The right amount of anxiety is ok however having too much anxiety can interfere with a person's life. Anxiety symptoms are real. They can include nausea, faintness, sweating, shaking, shortness of breath, rapid heartbeat, chest pains, worry, fear, restlessness.

Anxiety will go away once the trigger event is over. Anxiety can be a problem when you are confronted on a daily basis the trigger or event. For example, riding an elevator, going to work, driving in traffic. It can also be a problem when it is excessive or irrational dread of everyday situations.

People with anxiety disorder experience excessive fear and worry that are out of proportion to the situation. These feelings are more intense and last longer than normal feelings of anxiety.

People with anxiety disorder finds it to be difficult to control worry or stress. If anxiety interferes with your daily activities, then it is time to see your doctor or a mental health professional. Anxiety is treatable. Sometime mediations are needed and also see a therapist is a must for a while.

What causes anxiety? People with Mental illness such as depression and bi polar disorder can also have anxiety. It also can be a side effect of medications, life's events, runs in the family, sperate illness whether it is physical or psychological.

Panic disorder is different than anxiety.

Symptoms of a panic attack are the following:

- Fear

- Heart palpitations

- Pounding of the heart

- Fast heart rate

- Sweeting

- Trembling or shaking

- Shortness of breath

- Smothering

- Feeling of doom.

Panic attacks can be brought on suddenly.

Sometimes a person cannot actually tell what

caused the panic attack. Other times it may be

due to life situations. For example, a person is

in a car accident. Going back into the car can

bring on a panic attack. It is the fear of getting

into another accident. People with panic attacks

usually avoid places where a panic attack has

occurred.

Chapter 20

Stages of Recovery

Recovery is a process of steps we need to

take to get on our individual role of recovery.

On the next page are the Twelve Steps of

Depressed Anonymous:

The Twelve Steps of Depressed Anonymous

1. We admitted that we were powerless
    over depression that our lives had
    become unmanageable.

2. Came to believe that a Power greater
    than ourselves could restore us to sanity.

3. Made a decision to turn our will and our
    lives over to the care of God, as we
    understood him.

4. Made a searching and fearless moral

inventory of ourselves.

5. Admitted to God, to ourselves and to

another human being the exact nature of

our wrongs.

6. We are entirely ready to have God

remove all these defects of character.

7. Humbly asked Him to remove our short

comings.

8. Made a list of all persons we had harmed

and became willing to make amends to

them all.

9. Made direct amends to such people

wherever possible, except when to do so

would injure them or others.

10. Continued to take a personal inventory
and when we were wrong promptly
admitted it.

11. Sought through prayer and meditation
to improve our conscious contact with
God as we understood Him, praying only
for knowledge of His will for us and the
power to carry it out.

12. Having had a spiritual awakening as the
result of these steps, we tried to carry the

message to other depressed persons and
to practice principles in all our affairs.

The first and important step we need to take is that of acceptance. We need to accept our illness.

It took me time to recover from my mental illness. I still have to take medications which is ok by me. I had to work each step of the 12 steps. There are times I have to go back to them. I wrote a personal inventory for my good points and my bad points. This was useful to help me to work on the negative side of me. Read each of the 12 steps and start to work on them today. This is just one part of the road to recovery.

Chapter 21

Beginning your Journey to Recovery

There are three important things you need to

do to start your journey. The first is find

yourself a good medical doctor. It is important

that you let your doctor know all the medications

you are taking. It is a good idea to have a

physical examination once a year. The second is

managing your medications. Learn what each

medication if for, how they work and if there are

any side effects. A good idea is like I have is a

weekly pill organizer. Once a week I fill up the

organizer by day, morning, afternoon and

evenings. This makes it easier for you to

determine if you missed taking a dose. Throw

away any old medications that you are no longer

taking. It is a very good idea not to drink any

alcohol while you are on any type of

medications whether it is physical or

psychological. If you develop any new side

effect be sure to contact your doctor. The third

important task you should take is find yourself a

good psychotherapist. By working with your

therapist, the both of you can find a good

treatment plan to take that will work for you.

Just as important to keep your doctor

appointments it is also important to keep

appointments with your therapist.

You will learn what you need to do each day to stay on the road to recovery. It is important that you monitor and respond to symptoms. As time goes by you will be able to determine what triggers may have cause your symptoms to increase. You will be able to detect warning signs of an episode and symptoms that indicate you may be heading for trouble.

Use some of the following tools that may help you to develop your skills in knowing ahead of time of an early on-set to your illness:

1. Daily routines you need to do such as eating three meals, get adequate sleep,

take all your medications and exercise
regularly.

2. Plan a head of time coping skills you can
    use with events that can trigger your
    symptoms. For an example if you have an
    argument with a friend of yours or an
    unexpected bill comes in the mail learn
    ways to cope so you do not trigger any
    symptoms.

3. Spot early warning signs such as changes
    is sleep, depression, mania, anxiety. This
    could indicate your symptoms are getting
    worse.

4. If you start to isolate, suicidal thoughts, reckless behavior could be the beginning signs of real trouble.

5. Make a response plan for dealing with warning and/or trouble signs. This will help you to take action quickly, so you can get the necessary help to stabilize your situation. You may want to include in your response plan to call your doctor, therapist, family or friend right away.

Wellness Toolbox

You want to include the following in your

Wellness Toolbox:

- Find and attend a local support group

  regularly

- Talk to your therapist, doctor on a regular

  basis especially if you are experiencing

  early warning signs of an episode.

- Talk to a friend often especially when you

  are having a difficult time.

- Exercise on a regular basis to help you

  reduce stress.

- Go for a walk everyday

- Do some fun and creative activity.

- Keep a journal of your feelings and thoughts.

- Make a daily planning calendar.

- Try to avoid caffeine, sugar and salted foods.

- Keep a list of your current medications.

You also should develop a plan should your symptoms become so severe and or dangerous where you are unable to make decisions for yourself. In your Crisis Plan you would want to include your supporters such as doctors, therapist, family or friends. Write down their role in your life and their phone numbers.

Below is a list of symptoms you may have which indicates you may need for your supporters to make decision on your behalf:

- Thoughts of suicide

- Refusal to eat

- Abusive or violent behavior

- Thoughts of harming yourself or someone else.

- Not able to sleep

- Severe depression

- Have written down directions to notify your employer in the event you should need to be hospitalized.

- Written down directions for care of your children and/or pets should you need to be hospitalized.

- Have a list of what you need your supporters to do for you in the event of a crisis.

It is a good idea for you to have the above written down and give it to all your supporters. You may also want to have an advance directive written up. This is basically the same as the above only it is more detail.

Develop a wellness lifestyle. Stay well by utilize all of the above to maintain your wellness. Work on improving your self-esteem.

Change your negative thoughts into positive

ones. Enhance your life with things that makes

you feel good. This may include any pets you

may have, music you like to listen to or activities

you like to do. Continue to attend any self-help

groups and go to meetings. Eat well balanced

meals. Get plenty of rest and exercise on a daily

basis. Remember get help right away before

your symptoms gets worse. Enjoy life!

Chapter 22

Develop a Recovery Plan

Recovery is possible with everyone. It is a process of treatment on an ongoing process which happens over time. The first step in recovery is admit to yourself that you need help and you cannot do this on your own. Get help right away. There is no shame in admitting you have a mental illness and need help. Seek out a psychiatrist is the first thing you want to do. Perhaps he or she can recommend a good therapist.

My recovery plan is:

1. Recognize early warning signs of depression.

2. Call your doctor or therapist should your symptoms get worse.

3. Be sure you are taking all your medications as prescribed.

4. Do relaxation exercises.

5. Exercise even if it means just going for a walk.

6. Journal.

7. Get plenty of light.

8. Think positive.

9. Simplify your day.

10.Make a list of things you need to do.

11.What activities you should avoid when you are having early warning signs of depression.

12.Keep up with your personal hygiene.

The four dimensions of recovery are health, home, purpose, and community. Make good choices that support your physical and emotional wellbeing. Have a good and stable place to live. If you are living where there is nothing but problems work on moving to a more less stressful place to live. Keep active during the day.

This includes meaningful daily activities,

such as a job, going to school,

volunteering, caring for your family or

pet. Build relationships and social

networks that will provide you with

support. Perhaps you can find a good

self-help center or a group for people with

depression. Focus on staying well.

Chapter 23

Closing Thoughts

I have lived with mental illness for twenty years now. I have had my bad days and then I have had my good days. At least now with all the education and experience I have had over the years I know what I am dealing with. Even to the present I still have my times where that old depression haunts me. I learned how to live with it and how to cope when those days come back at me. A lot of the experience I have had over the years are from my own mental illness. I have gone to many seminars, conferences, and groups. I am ¾ the way to get my associates degree in psych and rehab. If you have just been diagnosed with some form of mental illness it is not the end of the world. Just learn how to deal with it and live each day. Enjoy the good days you have and seek help on those hard days that may come. Medication is a very important tool for all types of illnesses whether it is physical or psychological.

There is day light at the end of each tunnel just keep following the light. You too will be soon out of the dark tunnel. Trust in God that He will see you through it.

Best wishes to all of you

Bruce Dolan Smith

Credits

www.dictionary.com

www.mental-illness-resourses.com

Living Without Depression & Manic Depression
by Mary Ellen Copeland, M.S.

http://www.activebeat.com/your-health/15-
natural-remedies-for-treating-depression
08/02/2017 1:51am

http://www.the-guided-meditation-site.com/5-
minute-morning-meditation-script.html
08/02/2017

Substance Abuse and Mental Health Services

Administration, Center for Mental Health

Services

https://www.mentalhealth.gov/basics/recovery/in

dex.html

www.dbsalliance.org